RETIREMENT IS A **FULL-TIME JOB**
AND YOU'RE THE BOSS!

RETIREMENT IS A FULL-TIME JOB
AND YOU'RE THE BOSS!

Bonnie Louise Kuchler

WILLOW CREEK PRESS

Published by Willow Creek Press
P.O. Box 147, Minocqua, Wisconsin 54548

For information on other Willow Creek Press titles,
call 1-800-850-9453

Photo Credits: p2 © Steve Kershaw/Alamy; p6 © Juniors Bildarchiv/Alamy; p9 © P. Wegner/Arco Images GmbH/Alamy
p10,11 © Meyers / blickwinkel/Alamy; p13 © Aspix/Alamy; p14 © Peltomaeki/blickwinkel/Alamy; p17 © Shangara Singh / Alamy;
p18 © TUNS/Arco Images GmbH/Alamy; p21 © Ron Kimball / kimballstock; p22 © C. Steimer/Arco Images GmbH/Alamy;
p25 © Craig Ellenwood/Alamy; p26 © Image Source Pink/Alamy; p29 © Coston Stock/Alamy;
p30 © Richard du Toi/Gallo Images/Alamy; p32,33; © Johnny Johnson/Alaska Stock LLC.; p34 © Gary Randall/Kimball Stock;
p37 © H. Reinhard/Arco Images GmbH/Alamy; p38 © Huetter/blickwinkel/Alamy; p41 © Peltomaeki/blickwinkel/Alamy;
p42 © tbkmedia.de/Alamy; p45 © Lisa & Mike Husar/TeamHusar.com; p46 Tui De Roy/Minden Pictures;
p49 © Liedmann/blickwinkel/Alamy; p50 © Walz/blickwinkel/Alamy; p53 © Stefan Meyers/ardea.com;
p54; © John W. Warden/Stock Connection Distribution/Alamy; p56,57 © Natalia Bratslavsky/Alamy;
p58 © Wermter/blickwinkel/Alamy; p61 © M. Klindwort/Arco Images GmbH/Alamy; p62,63 © fotototo/blickwinkel/Alamy;
p65 © Corey Hochachka/Design Pics Inc./Alamy; p66 © Poelking/blickwinkel/Alamy; p68,69 © Reagan Pannell/Alamy;
p70 © M. Watson/ardea.com; p73 © Laule/blickwinkel/Alamy; p74 © Travis Rowan/Alamy; p76,77 © Pieper/blickwinkel/Alamy;
p78 © Duncan Usher/ardea.com; p81 © Layer/blickwinkel/Alamy; p82 © Lohmann/blickwinkel/Alamy;
p84,85 © Steven Kazlowski/Kimball Stock; p86 © Lisa & Mike Husar/TeamHusar.com; p89 © TUNS/Arco Images GmbH/Alamy;
p90 © Kaufung/blickwinkel/Alamy; p93 © Radius Images/Alamy; p94,95 © Puppetti/blickwinkel/Alamy

Printed in China

Retirement is not a sunset;
it is the dawn of your time...

So, grab your
senior discount coupons,
your fishing pole, your golf clubs,
your tennis racket, your hat,
your glasses, your arch supports,
a nap,
and go
CELEBRATE!

If retirement is a brand new journey,
a nap is a good first step.

If people were meant to pop out of bed,
we'd all sleep in toasters.
—Garfield

Retirement is a season for new pursuits
and favorite hobbies—
like puttering in the yard.

Bread feeds the body, indeed, but flowers feed also the soul.
—the Koran

You'll have time to go
fishing with friends...

A bad day of fishing is better
than a good day of work.
—Bumper sticker

...or go fishing for
golf balls.

I swim a lot. It's either that or buy a new golf ball.
—Bob Hope

You'll have time to watch neighbors...

The cure for boredom is curiosity.
There is no cure for curiosity.
—Dorothy Parker

...and their visitors.

Curiosity... most frequently we wish not to know, but to talk.
—Blaise Pascal

You'll finally have time to stretch out in the grass and contemplate the clouds.

Indeed, it is one of the enjoyments of retirement that
you are able to drift through the day at your own pace.
—Kazuo Ishiguro

You can enjoy sleeping in—
or out—
without a twinge of guilt.

I'm now equipped with a snooze button.
—Denis Norden

A retired husband is often
a wife's full-time job.

—Ella Harris

Along with retirement comes a subtle relaxing of the mind.

Age is strictly a case of mind over matter.
If you don't mind, it doesn't matter.
—Mark Twain

You may find that you misplace things.

There are three signs of old age: Loss of memory...
I forget the other two.
—Red Skelton

You might misplace your inhibitions.

There is something awe-inspiring in someone who has lost all inhibitions.
—F. Scott Fitzgerald

You might misplace your self-control.

It's all right letting yourself go,
as long as you get yourself back.
—Mick Jagger

You might even misplace your house.

First you forget names, then you forget faces,
then you forget to pull your zipper up,
then you forget to pull your zipper down.
—Leo Rosenberg

Just when your memory starts to play tricks on you, you'll have new things to remember. Like where you put your teeth.

One of the signs of old age is that you have to carry your senses around in your handbag—glasses, hearing aids, dentures...
—Kurt Strauss

Thankfully,
"Laughter doesn't require teeth."
—Bill Newton

Age usually comes fully loaded
with maturity, wisdom, and keen insight.
But sometimes age comes along all by itself.

The older I grow the more I distrust the
familiar doctrine that age brings wisdom.
—H.L. Mencken

Being retired means you can learn to play again.

Years wrinkle the skin, but to give up
enthusiasm wrinkles the soul.
—Luella F. Phelan

You might want to pace yourself.

I decided to take an aerobics class for seniors. I bent, twisted,
gyrated, jumped up and down, and perspired for an hour.
But, by the time I got my leotards on, the class was over.
—Unknown

Don't let a few creaks and groans stop you.
Enjoy the grandkids!

I'll keep going until my face falls off.
—Barbara Cartland

Dust off your
dancing shoes!

I'm getting into swing dancing. Not on purpose.
Some parts of my body are just prone to swinging.

—Unknown

Go for a roll in the hay!

Of all the faculties, the last to leave us is sexual desire.
That means that long after wearing bifocals and hearing aids,
we'll still be making love. We just won't know with whom.
—Jack Paar

The problem is not so much resisting temptation as finding it.

—Los Angeles Times

Now that you're retired
you may notice little changes in your body.

It's scary when you start making the
same noises as your coffeemaker.
—Unknown

Eyesight
is the first to go...

The only reason I wear my glasses is for little things,
like driving my car—or finding it.
—Woody Allen

...then
hearing.

Don't underestimate the value of doing
nothing, of just going along, listening to all
the things you can't hear, and not bothering.
—Winnie the Pooh

You may notice that the sides of your face now meet at the back of your head.

I knew I was going bald when it was
taking longer and longer to wash my face.
—Harry Hill

When you talk about "balance," you'll no longer be talking about juggling work and family.

They say the first thing to go... is your legs or your eyesight.
It isn't true. The first thing to go is parallel parking.
—Kurt Vonnegut

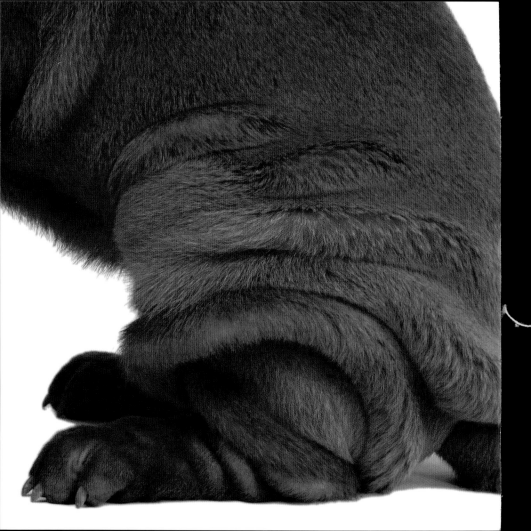

Eventually,
everything yields to gravity.

I have a furniture problem.
My chest has fallen into my drawers.
—Billy Casper

There is always a lot to be thankful for...
For example, I'm sitting here thinking
how nice it is that wrinkles don't hurt.

—Unknown

Being retired means no more alarm clocks or **bumper-to-bumper commutes.**

I'm not just retiring from the company,
I'm also retiring from my stress, my commute,
my alarm clock, and my iron.
—Hartman Jule

You can take the road
less traveled.

I don't want to get to the end of my life
and find that I lived just the length of it.
I want to have lived the width of it as well.
—Diane Ackerman

You can take off on
new adventures.

Like all great travelers, I have seen more than I remember,
and remember more than I have seen.

—Benjamin Disraeli

You can take a daily stroll with friends.

My grandmother started walking five miles a day
when she was sixty. She's ninety-three today
and we don't know where the hell she is.
—Ellen DeGeneres

You can take a refreshing swim.

Live in the sunshine, swim the sea, drink the wild air.
—Ralph Waldo Emerson

Or you can take the highway and
not even hear the honking behind you.

Retirement is when you want to see how long
your car will last, instead of how fast it will go.
—Unknown

It's nice to get out of the rat race,
but you have to learn to get along with
less cheese.

—Gene Perret

No doubt, you'll think up creative ways to spend time— without spending money.

I have enough money to last me the rest of my life—unless I have to buy something.
—Jackie Mason

Fortunately, it is a privilege of retirement to **stop caring what people think.**

You can only hold your stomach in for so many years.
—Burt Reynolds

With so much free time, little things won't bother you the way they used to.

The longer I live, the more beautiful life becomes.
—Frank Lloyd Wright

Being retired means you can spend more time with your favorite people.

Cherish all your happy moments;
they make a fine cushion for old age.
—Booth Tarkington

Young people will draw
from your well of experience.

The great thing about getting older is that
you don't lose all the other ages you've been.
—Madeleine L'Engle

You may find that every day
you lived was setting the stage
for right now.

The prime of life is that fleeting time
between green and over-ripe.
—Cullen Hightower

Onward into your newfound
freedom!

Though it sounds absurd, it is true to say
I felt younger at sixty than I felt at twenty.
—Ellen Glasgow

Enjoy
the good life.